PROPERTY PROBLEM SOLVER

-

Has Your Property Become A Pain In Your Life?™ Part 2

"A solution to your pain could be on your doorstep"

LASHAI BEN SALMI & TRAY-SÉAN BEN SALMI

*AMAZON #1 BEST SELLER, AWARD WINNING AUTHORS
AS SEEN ON RADIO, NEWSPAPERS & TELEVISION*

PROPERTY PROBLEM SOLVER - Has Your Property Become A Pain In Your Life? ™ Part 2

Published by Stepping Stones Publishing in 2019

Copyright © Lashai Ben Salmi & Tray-Séan Ben Salmi 2019

Second Edition

The author asserts the moral right under the Copyright, Designs and Patents Act 1988 to be identified as the author of this work.

Cover Design by: Swiss Graphics

ISBN: 978-1-913310-06-6

'YOU' called this book to you because you desire a solution to your property problem and the pain of this has become unbearable beyond words. We live in an ever-changing world and you desire to be a part of the change that you wish to see in this world. Everything starts with an idea or concept in your mind. The idea or concept is then given form by taking aligned action. Then the magic begins to happen during the construction process and that process begins here and **now**!

This book is dedicated to people like you that have a burning desire to solve their PROPERTY PROBLEM and then go into life in pursuit of their DREAMS & ASPIRATIONS.

This book is not intended to provide personalised legal, financial or investment advice. The Author and the Publisher specifically disclaim any liability, loss and/or risk which is incurred therefore, directly or indirectly, of the use and application of any content of this work.

ACKNOWLEDGEMENTS

We would like to thank God for our abundance of wealth, health, happiness, opportunities and support in our lives! We would also like to take this opportunity to thank all of the amazing people that have supported us, guided us and taught us along our journey. We really and truly would not be where we are today if it was not for family, friends and priceless network of support.

We would also like to take this opportunity to acknowledge those of you who have delivered adversity to our lives, because this has made us stronger and inspired us to convert our adversities into empowerment. After all we are who we are today as a direct result of everything that we have experienced.

Foreword

I am delighted to write the foreword for PROPERTY PROBLEM SOLVER - Has Your Property Become A Pain In Your Life? ™ co-authored by Lashai and Tray-Sean Ben Salmi. Lashai and Tray-Sean are my mentees and I thoroughly enjoy observing them go from strength to strength in property and investment as a result of my teachings. I have recently retired as the founder and managing Director of a successful IFA/Mortgage Broking Practice, which I setup back in the late 80's and is known as Henderson Ponsford & Co, employing a team of 6 Brokers and support staff. It was in my teenage years when I discovered that I have an innate interest and a burning desire for knowledge in personal development. I knew then that I was to discover the secret behind our human potential. This book has been written with you in mind and with the aim to expand your awareness to an array of options that are on your doorstep if you are currently experiencing property problems. This book aims to empower you to get in touch with Lashai, Tray-Sean and myself to seek information about the options that are available to you. Establishing contact with us could help you to turn a bad situation around depending on your circumstances. Do not dig your head in sand, because ignoring all the warnings and failing to contact us could have a disastrous impact on your life.

This book encourages you to get in touch if you are struggling to cope and seeking a quick sale to enable you to have a fresh start.

Douglas Ponsford
Author, Investor, Public Speaker and Mentor

CONTENTS

Just imagine how you'll feel as you finish reading
the last page of this book......

INTRODUCTION

We wrote this book with you in mind, with the primary intention to ***SOLVE YOUR PROPERTY PROBLEMS*** and to encourage you to go on and live your dreams; no matter how bad things may currently seem.

While buying a property can be an exciting mile stone in your life, but the question is what happens when that property becomes a nightmare pain in your life?

If you wish to find a remedy to soothe the pain that your property is causing in your life then we suggest that you read this book and contact us for more information.

Go ahead and take a deep breath and rest assure because you are not alone. Myself (Lashai Ben Salmi), my brother Tray-Sean Ben Salmi together with our property mentor Douglas Ponsford are passionate ***PROPERTY PROBLEM SOLVERS***.

Our mentor Douglas Ponsford is a renowned property investor with over 30 years experience within the property investment industry. Together we are determined* to ***SOLVE YOUR PROPERTY PROBLEMS*** and transform your life (*subject to your individual circumstances that will need to be discussed in more depth).

How would it feel should the unfortunate happen?

Will solving your property problem enable you to release old ties and reclaim energy so you can go into your own life?

Do you struggle to sleep at night due to stress?

What impact has your property problems had on your health?

What impact has your property problems had on your finances?

What impact has your property problems had on your career/business?

What impact has your property problems had on your relationships with friends and family?

How bad is your property problem?

How long have you been feeling the pain due to your property problem?

How long have you been hiding your head in the sand, hoping that your property problem would just go away?

Are you willing to do whatever it takes in order to ***SOLVE YOUR PROPERTY PROBLEM NOW***?

How would it feel to be able to have a last minute opportunity to solve your property problem?

Take a moment to visualise how different your life will be once you *SOLVE YOUR PROPERTY PROBLEM*.

In essence, do you desire to sell your property as quickly as possible, and are you less concerned with getting the full value of the property?

You may find yourself in a situation where you are seeking a quick sale. If this is the case, please do not hesitate to contact us.

IT'S GOOD TO TALK

Are you good at expressing yourself?

Talking to someone about the reality of the pain that your property is causing and about what might happen in the future can be daunting and many people avoid having these conversations. However, talking to someone could help you to expand your awareness on options that could help you to make an informed decision and have the peace of mind of knowing that you have at least taken aligned action to explore all your options.

Within our network, we have often heard people say that divorce is leaving hundreds of thousands of people facing an uncertain financial future, because they do not get the right advice when a marriage ends. One in three are unable to make any further savings after a split while two in five have no clear idea what settlement they'll receive as part of their divorce and two-thirds of divorcees expect they will be forced to rely on the State pension in retirement.

We have grown to realise that it is almost impossible for a couple to go through a divorce without leaving themselves worse off because they are having to carve out two households out of one. The right advice can help ensure a better and smoother settlement for both parties. To our dismay, we have also learned that one in four women choose to go down the road of a DIY divorce and taken no help in sorting out their finances. Which means that these women not only given up rights to their husband's pension provision, but also stopped paying into their own pension and may have lost contact with savings they had. We overheard a conversation where a person was being educated on the fact that couples should keep some assets in their own names even in a healthy relationship, because this will allow both husband and wife to use their individual tax allowances, which means that should one spouse die the other will have ready access to cash.

Interesting right?

They went on to explain that, if you leave the entire family finances in only the husband's or the wife's name that could be extremely risky if a relationship turns sour (we are not financial advisors so for more information please do contact a financial advisor) not having assets in each of their own names can become extremely costly.

We have heard so many stories about families that have be torn apart due to the heartfelt realities that can come to surface in relation to family rebate cases. In cases such as these family members merely desire to sell their property as quickly as possible to get hold of their cash inheritance.

We often hear about stories of people in serious debt and needing to sell their property/properties as quickly as possible to repay debt with the aim to avoid bankruptcy.

And there are those stories of people who desire to sell their home to merely downsize or move aboard and they often seek a quick sell too.

In some cases landlords are having their lives turned upside down, enduring months, sometimes years, of stress to regain access to that most basic of human rights, their own property. It's not just tenants. Some landlords do not have large portfolios, they are your everyday man, woman, grandmother, grandfather, mother, father, friend and/or couples who have seen the very worst that the rental market can offer.

Their properties used to be well maintained, equipped, and a considerable source of pride to them in a number of ways. Then one day their pride and joy turned into their pain and often this is due to renting the property to someone in a difficult situation, on the personal recommendation of family and/or a friend out of a compassionate desire to help someone out of a difficult situation. Only to find that this person goes on to systematically destroy the landlords life.

The once well-furnished and well-presented property was reduced to an unrecognisable disrepair shell, barely a fraction of what it once was.

You only need to do a Google on this topic to discover the total nightmare that some landlords have experienced. For example, windows nailed shut, property stolen, huge holes in walls/ceilings/floors, exterior/interior doors kicked in, appliances damaged beyond repair, landlords family members threatened, neighbours alienated and abused and the once presentable property has merely become a distant memory of the past. We cannot begin to imagine the immense deep-rooted pain that YOU and others people face when their property becomes a pain in their lives. It is so unfortunate for anyone to have to endure the above. Just know that you are not alone, please do not hesitate to contact us.

After all the difference that could make the difference is reaching out to establish all your options and that could be the difference between peace of mind and a situation that can test your sanity, finances, health and relationships etc.

LANDLORD

Are you a landlord?

If you are a man or woman who rents out land, a building, or accommodation.

We respect the fact that at times, you may not be making as much money as you initially intended on a particular property. Therefore, you desire to and/or feel forced to sell as quickly as possible.

You might do this for a number of reasons perhaps the property is continuously depreciating in value, or due to the maintenance consistently exceeding the amount of money that you generate in rent. This can then lead to you being out of pocket each month.

Just know that you're not alone so do not hesitate to contact us so we can discuss your options.

HEIRS

Are you an heir?

If you are a person legally entitled to a property and/or rank of another due to the death of a relative. The person's assets can be passed down to you as the heirs through the will. One of the main assets is usually the home of the deceased.

We have grown to learn that the heir or heirs often do not want the property and often choose to sell it.

Therefore, we can understand that in these situations that you may desire to sell the property as quick as possible mainly because no one is living in the property, therefore you are losing money on it. So the longer that you hold on to the property the more you may have to pay for the insurance, maintenance and tax etc. Not to mention the emotional strain of having to cope with relatives who are anticipating a rapid sale.

FORECLOSURE

Are you an homeowner under threat of foreclosure?

You may be facing the traumatic reality of awaiting a foreclosure on your home. The action of taking possession of a mortgaged property as a result of not being able to keep up to date with your mortgage payments.

Unfortunately, there has been a major increase in home foreclosures due to a host of root causes which can vary from individual to individual.

We can appreciate the immense stress that you may be under due to your current reality because you cannot keep up to date with your mortgage payments, not to mention the added stress of knowing that you are very close to being foreclosed on by the bank. Due to this fast approaching reality we can appreciate that you are feeling extremely eager to sell your property to avoid foreclosure. You may find yourself in a situation where you are seeking a quick sale. If this is the case, please do not hesitate to contact us.

BANK IN POSSESSION of REOs

Is the bank in possession of REOs (Real Estate Owned)?

When a house is foreclosed upon, it typically becomes eligible for sale at a foreclosure auction.

In the unfortunate event of the property not selling at auction, the lender (this is usually a bank) keeps possession of the property. While the bank holds onto the property while they are rapidly losing money not to mention the that the property is always under threat of vandalism due to being empty.

In such cases the lender wants the property off of their hands as quickly as possible and is usually willing to negotiate in order to secure a quick sale.

RELOCATING FOR A NEW JOB

Are you relocating to seek a new job?

Are you relocating to start a new job?

With our ever-changing economy, jobs can be hard to come by and at times you may find yourself needing to relocate in order to seek or secure a new job.

If this relates to you, go ahead and take a deep breath. Perhaps you've recently been offered a new job or you're currently seeking a new job and you need to sell your property as quickly as possible so you can move to a new area to either seek or start a new job. We can totally understand that time is of the essence, therefore a quick sale could enable you to relocate as soon as possible because getting the sale over and done with would enable you to embrace your new life. You may find yourself in a situation where you are seeking a quick sale. If this is the case, please do not hesitate to contact us.

UNEMPLOYMENT

Are unemployed?

Are you going to be made unemployed?

Are you stressed due to being long term unemployed?

You may be feeling a deep sense of fear of losing your home due to unexpectedly losing your job or long-term unemployment.

You may be praying for a quick sale and/or hoping to find a new job even if the income is lower for a short period of time.

As a result of this circumstance we can totally understand that it is beginning to become impossible to maintain your monthly mortgage payments not to mention additional expenses.

You may often find yourself trying to hide your head in the sand, due to the fast approaching reality of you losing your home and this scares you daily.

The chances are that if you do not find employment soon you may have to sell your home and purchase a less expensive one or you may lose your home if you keep hiding your head in the sand.

We can understand if you desire to sell your home quickly to finally put an end to the never ending:

- Stress
- Sleepless nights
- Mood swings
- Headaches
- Head fog
- Chest pains
- Depression
- Anxiety and so much more

you may find yourself in a situation where you are seeking a quick sale. If this is the case, please do not hesitate to contact us.

DIVORCE & SEPARATION

Are you divorced?

Are you separated?

Are you thinking of separating or divorcing?

If you are currently in the process of a divorce or a separation it can be an extremely stressful, vicious and a deeply emotionally draining process due to couples solicitors battling against each other with the aim to finalise the divorce.

If you happen to be the partner that is rewarded the house and you find yourself desiring to sell the house quickly before your significant other tries to renegotiate the assets. Or you may find yourself having to sell the house together and splitting the half of the profit with your ex. Not to mention the fact that by this time things between you and your ex might be disorganized, not to mention the lack of rapport that will have a huge impact on the way you both choose to communicate.

Due to the above as so much more, you may have a desire to sell the house and get the process over and done with as soon as possible.

You may find yourself in a situation where you are seeking a quick sale. If this is the case, please do not hesitate to contact us.

EXPECTING A BABY

Are you expecting a baby?

Firstly, if you are pregnant, we would like to take this opportunity to congratulate you. We would also like to wish you a healthy and safe pregnancy and delivery.

A pregnancy can totally transform the dynamics of your life, not to mention the fact that expecting a new baby may mean that you and your family will have to move into a larger home to accommodate your expanding family needs.

For some there is still time to sell your home and relocate and for others there's little to no time at all because you're in the final stages of your pregnancy. Therefore, a quick sell will enable you to sell your current home, giving you the peace of mind of being able to settle your family into your new home in time for the arrival of your precious baby.

We can only imagine the emotional and physical stress that you will have to go through when having to deal with selling your home, seeking a suitable home and getting settled into a new home on top of the added responsibility of having to take care of a newborn and gaining adequate rest for yourself too.

We can imagine that you'd prefer to be spending quality time with your precious new baby instead of

having to worry about home hunting, selling you're
your home, relocating etc.

Take a moment to visualize your desired outcome
when your precious new baby arrives.

- How do you desire to spend you days?

- Where do you desire to live?

- What are the pros and cons of selling your
  home now?

- What are the pros and cons of selling your
  home following the birth of your baby?

you may find yourself in a situation where you are
seeking a quick sale. If this is the case, please do not
hesitate to contact us.

DISREPAIR

Is your home in a serious state of disrepair?

Nowadays many home owners experience financial constraints from time to time which can then lead to them neglecting your home maintenance responsibilities in order to reduce outgoings with the aim to make monthly mortgage payments and additional financial obligations.

If this relates to you, then you may find that you've essentially made your home into an unappealing property for those who are seeking to purchase a home that they could move straight in without needing to do any renovations.

In such cases you may find that most will not want to buy the home, especially for the price it is listed at. Therefore, you may find yourself in a situation where you are seeking a quick sale. If this is the case, please do not hesitate to contact us.

DERELICT PROPERTY

Are you an owner of a derelict property?

If you are an owner of a derelict property, we can totally understand that you may be feeling a sense of discomfort due to being in an undesirable position.

You may also be feeling as if you will never be able to sell your property.

Try to maintain faith as there may still be hope providing that there are no permanent structural damages.

It may be a good idea to schedule an inspector to verify that there are no permanent structural issues to enable you to confidently reassure potential buyers otherwise you may find yourself feeling stuck with some major problems.

You may find yourself in a situation where you are seeking a quick sale. If this is the case, please do not hesitate to contact us.

TAKE ALIGNED ACTION TO SOLVE YOUR PROPERTY PROBLEMS

Please do not hesitate to contact us to discuss your options to SOLVE YOUR PROPERTY PROBLEMS

Facebook Group:
Property Problem Solver – Has Your Property
Become A Pain In Your Life?

Instagram:
propertyproblemsolvers

Twitter:
@propertypains

Email:
resolvemypropertypains@gmail.com

EXCLUSIVE BONUS - SOME FOOD FOR THOUGHT TO PLANT THE SEED FOR YOUR DREAMS

WE BELIEVE IN YOU

We believe you can fly, we believe you can touch the sky. Simply think about your dreams throughout your day, and you shall witness changes in your life. Visualise yourself immersed in your dreams. Live your life with purpose and passion at your core. Begin your dance with the universe right **now**. Simply allow your dreams to take you to new heights. Plant your seeds today for a brighter future tomorrow.

Remember you don't grow the dream, your dreams grow you.

- Expect support

- Expect a miracle, unexpected pleasantries in abundance

- Expect a cheque or even several cheques

- Expect expanded awareness and progress

- Expect financial and time freedom

Simply believe in yourself and all will be well

Believe
in yourself
&
you will be
Unstoppable

BECKONING YOU

We am confident that you will find the following

questions useful:

- Where do you get stuck (list 3)?

- How long have you felt stuck?

- What is keeping you stuck (list 3)?

- Which three things will move you forward?

- How will these three things move you forward?

- When do you desire a breakthrough?

- How will you **know** that you've had a **breakthrough** (describe your desired outcome)?

- Where are you **now** in life?

- What needs to happen in order to bridge the gap?

- What do you wish to be remembered for?

- From 1 – 10 how motivated are you about attaining your desired outcome(s)?

- What would make you lose motivation?

- What will assist to maintain motivation?

- What would increase your motivation?

- Who are you really?

- What do you value most?

- What will you leave behind when you change?

- What will you gain?

- What are you passionate about?

- What are your weaknesses?

- What are your strengths?

- What is your vision?

- Can you make a living from your passion/purpose?

- What do you intend to transform?

- What are your values in relation to money, success and relationships?

- What are your beliefs in relation to money, success and relationships?

- What 5 things are most important to you in life?

- Why do you want freedom - remember the bigger the 'Why?' the easier the 'how?'

- What are you going to do right **NOW**?

- What were you pretending not to k**now** in order to believe that you didn't have the ability to pursue your dream(s)?

- What have you learning about yourself?

- What have you learned about others?

- What have you learned about life?

- What will you transform **now**?

- How do you k**now**?

- How much do you desire change?

- When will you TAKE ALIGNED ACTION?

Where in the past your old problems and limiting beliefs would have held you back – notice how you are looking at the world through new eyes. Your awareness has expanded, and the good news is that this is only the beginning. We wish you every

success within your life journey.

THE IMPORTANCE OF SLEEP

Do you have a healthy sleep pattern?

Set an intention to take a warm bath after putting your dependents to bed.

Add a couple of drops of chamomile or lavender oil into your bath and then simply relax and enjoy.

Go straight to bed - the increase in temperature combined with the oils will improve your circulation and naturally cause your body to relax.

Did you **know:**

- Missing a single night of sleep, despite being health reduces your immune-systems activity by at least 30%?

- If you are deprived of sleep for a total of 36 hours you increase your chances of depression by 60% and it will also affect your abilities such as judgement, logic and reasoning.

- We all require at least 8 hours sleep to recharge.

WHO'S TO BLAME?

Do you often blame others?

Whenever we point a finger, there are always three fingers pointing back at us. When a crisis is at hand, no matter how big or small, whether it is a question of loss of earnings, loss of limbs, the end of a relationship, loss of life or simply loss of face. That is not the time to seek someone to blame.

One ought to set about alleviating it as quickly and a most profoundly as we can. When all has been repaired and set right, we then look to causes and effects and perhaps learn from the event(s) which took place. I strongly believe that this is the principle that can indeed assist us within our life journey – I truly believe that this is the difference that makes the difference.

As you can be right or you can BE HAPPY!

I believe change is always happening, and there is always progress, development and forward movement even when there appears to be none.

Where in the past your old problems may have hindered you or held you back, notice how you are seeing things differently.

Your awareness is expanding and as a result, your reality is changing and it feels great – right?

Yes or No?

- Where in your life could you learn to simply be patient?

- What have you given up on prematurely?

- What would need to happen in order for you to fully comprehend the importance on seeing things through?

- How do you know?

- How might this relate to your journey?

- How do you **know**?

- What positive learnings did you gain?

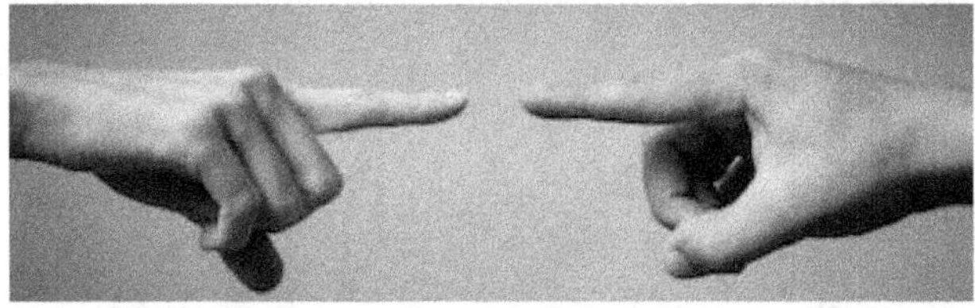

HOW DOES THIS RELATE TO YOUR JOURNEY?

I absolutely love stories, allow me to share this one with you:

I PLANTED A SEED

Ms Smith: Hi There, I'm Ms Smith. I am a lone parent mother of four and work part time in a school. I often experience a feeling of stress and desperation because I'm quite convinced nothing in my life has changed over the past 7 years. I've tried several times to setup in business, but things never workout.

I planted a seed – this morning I looked at the very spot with laser beam focus and nothing has appeared to have changed. The soil still looks unhampered. I've looked at it for days and days and come away thinking that it was a total waste of time planting my seed – because nothing appears to be happening.

There's absolutely no change, nothing, not a single change - the seed hasn't began to pout, nothing at all. Whatever I touch becomes a disaster, I doubt that it has changed shape beneath the soil because I cannot see any changes above. I'll continue to water and feed it for a while... as... I so hope that it will start to grow.

Us (Lashai & Tray): If you are to extend your perception, awareness and comprehension ever so slightly, you might become aware of the absolute eruption of change that is taking place inside the seed coat as the small embryonic plant is in fact experiencing an intricate storm of change: ordering, feeding and growth, which in turn become ever more defined, matured, complex and arranged day by day. One day, and we know not when, the seed that appeared to be laying so motionless for so very long and appeared to be doing absolutely nothing. Nonetheless, beneath the soil the seed will begin to change physically. The seed coat will crack, and the roots will emerge, and the stem will eventually penetrate the soil surface'

Ms Smith: As I opened my eyes, I felt overwhelmed with defeat after sleeping through the alarm. Immediately after breakfast the children began to quarrel. I felt as if my entire day would be a complete nightmare.

It had been several weeks since I entered our garden and I totally forgot about the seed that I had planted. Therefore, I decided to venture into my garden –

and I felt overwhelmed with joy. Yippee, yippee, yippee finally there was change – despite previous occasions when there appeared to be none. To my dismay, there it was...

I saw the primary stages of growth. I am so glad that my seed is showing signs of growth. Maybe I was wrong after all. Just when I had given in and allowed nature to take its course... changed happened and at that very moment I realised...

The questions is, what seed will you choose to plant today and simply surrender to the natural organic process?

WHAT'S YOUR
STORY

EXCLUSIVE BONUS ENTRY FOM SABRINA BEN SALMI

YOU ARE ENOUGH

*Good company in a journey makes the way seem
shorter. — Izaak Walton*

I am absolutely exhilarated about sharing Lone
Parenthood – You Are Enough with you.

I can still remember sitting down at home in our
spacious open plan three-bedroom home, the back
doors were open and the beautiful sunshine was
beaming hot and there was a lovely warm breeze
constantly coming in. With my one-year old son
wrapped around my neck while I was typing away
giving birth to Lone Parenthood – Essential Tips on
How To Create The Life You Deserve.

I can certainly say that I have learned so much in
my life journey since that very day. I am so in love
with the continuous organic unfoldment of life, the
contrast, the unexplainable encounters, the sweat,
the tears, the attachments, the fears, the discomfort,
the moments of sadness and despair, the unexpected
pleasantries in abundance and so much more. It is
such a deeply profound feeling to know that its
these very teachings within this book that took me
from feeling unworthy to a sense of self love and
Dreaming Big Together as a family and so much
more.

That which initially presented as a so-called pain, has gone on to become the premise for our thriving. I have come to realise that it was merely contrast and has now become our blessings beyond words. I have certainly learned that one can choose to grow through life or go through life. One thing that I truly believe is that life is a journey of market research and what you choose to do with the data is up to you.

The question is what will you choose?
You are enough, therefore:

-		Take the gift of life seriously and convey gratitude

-		No explanation needed

-		You have nothing to prove to others

-		You are unique, so there is no competition

-		Take care of yourself

-		Pursue your deepest dreams and desires

-		Know that you are worthy

-		Maintain faith and focus on thriving

-		Take a deep breath and fully reconnect with your inner core

-       Stop rushing, get into alignment and then life will come to you

-       Trust yourself

-       Trust your intuition

-       Give up the belief that you have to work hard to create your desired outcomes

-       You are growing through life

-       When contrast presents, choose to learn the lesson that it has come to teach you

-       You can choose to be in the choice

-       Express yourself

-       Being vulnerable is the first step towards success

-       Meditate daily to allow you to reconnect

-       You are a unique gift to the world

-       You are loved and supported

-       Investing in yourself is always a good idea

-       There is no such thing as failure, only feedback

-        All contrast helps you to fine tune that which you do not desire in order to fine tune you

-        Just know that you are exactly where you need to be, simply surrender to the process

-        Stop settling for too little

-        Be in a state of gratitude

-        Your opinion matters

-        You make a difference

-        Forgive yourself, others and let go

-        Slow down and simply be fully present to this very moment, that's the difference that will make the difference

-        Allow yourself to become an excellent giver and an excellent receiver

-        Learn to fall in love with yourself. So much so that you enjoy being alone in silence listening to your inner being and align

-        You are a speaker and the world is your stage

-        You are an artist and life is your canvas

- You are a musician and life will respond to your unique rhythm

- Surrender to the enigma of life, to allow flow

- Life has its seasons (spring, summer, autumn and winter) therefore learn your unique time when your soil turns, seeding stage, watering stage and harvesting stage

- Know that people are in your life for a reason, a season or a lifetime

- You are an author and the pen is in your hands

- Take the gift of life seriously and convey gratitude for all aspects of your life as often as possible

- Just know that you are exactly where you need to be, simply surrender to the process

- Stop settling for too little

- Acknowledge, appreciate and support those who support you within your life journey

- Slow down and simply be fully present to this very moment, that's the differnce that will make the difference

-       Redefine success according to you

-       You are worthy

-       Be still, just know that life will come to you

-       Forgive yourself

-       Forgive others

-       Say "How does it get any better than this?"
as often as possible

-       Convey gratitude for yourself and others

-       Know that your emotions are your internal
guidance system

-       Honor your needs and desires

-       All problems are problems of the mind
therefore all solutions are also solutions of the mind
too

-       Just know that contrast assists you to fine
tune that which you do not desire and empowers
you to powerfully pivot towards that which you
desire to experience

-       Walk in nature barefooted and allow
yourself to reconnect with nature

- When you have a negative thought simply say "Who does this belong to? I return to sender with consciousness attached"

- Use things and value people

- Acknowledge your strengths and weaknesses

- Stop trying so hard

- Being vulnerable is a strength

- Stop blaming others and tap into your inner power

- Expect unexpected pleasantries in abundance

- Learn to breathe deeply more often

- Take care of your business before you go into business

- Establish a network of support

- Know who to turn to during moments of need

- Asking for support is a strength, not a weakness

- Only the truth shall set you free

- Know thy self, love thy self and love thy neighbour

- Speak your truth

- Allow yourself to say yes, no, maybe or never when you feel to do so

- Allow yourself to be more playful

- Treat yourself more often

- You are not alone

- Pencil in some free time to allow yourself to go with the flow

- Create a not to do list

- Sing like no one is listening

- Make others see that there is something worthwhile in them

- Trust yourself

- Your inner compass will navigate you towards your dreams

- Talk like you've taken the truth serum

- It's possible for you too

-        Know that love, compassion and gratitude is always a good starting place

-        Believe in miracles

-        Invest in yourself

-        Hire a mentor

-        Ask for help when needed

-        Trust the process

-        Step outside of your comfort zone

-        Dance like no one is watching

-        Create systems and processes to make life run smoothly

-        Honor your thoughts by saying "thank you for sharing"

-        Stop trying to impress, friends, family and/or colleagues

-        Allow yourself to become an excellent giver and an excellent receiver

-        Learn to fall in love with yourself. So much so that you enjoy being alone in silence listening to your inner being and align

- When surrounded by crabs in the bucket trying to dilute your vision always respond saying "I'm just getting warmed up"

- In life you can either watch the movie, be in the movie and/or direct the movie

- Reconnect to your inner core

- Take aligned action

- Choose to be like water a adapt to life with flexibility

Embody the positive learnings for yourself and the future. Go ahead and take three deep breaths, with each breath that you take notice how relaxed you are becoming.

Now let's try this powerful breathing technique that our family mentor (Juanpa Barahona) taught us:
Take a slow and controlled deep breath to the count of 4 seconds. Now hold your breath for 4 seconds and then slowly exhale to the count of 4 seconds.

Excellent – well done, now let's go for 6 seconds. Take a slow and controlled deep breath to the count of 6 seconds. Now hold your breath for 6 seconds and then slowly exhale to the count of 6 seconds.

Excellent – well done, now let's go for 8 seconds.

Take a slow and controlled deep breath to the count
of 8 seconds. Now hold your breath for 8 seconds
and then slowly exhale to the count of 8 seconds.

Excellent – well done

Please allow me to share this poem with you, it's
called On Children and it inspired me to parent my
children the way I do today:

*"Your children are not your children. They are the
sons and daughters of Life's longing for itself. They
come through you but not from you, and though they
are with you yet they belong not to you. You may
give them your love but not your thoughts, for they
have their own thoughts. You may house their
bodies but not their souls, For their souls dwell in
the house of tomorrow, which you cannot visit, not
even in your dreams. You may strive to be like them,
but seek not to make them like you. For life goes not
backward nor tarries with yesterday. You are the
bows from which your children as living arrows are
sent forth. The archer sees the mark upon the path
of the infinite, and He bends you with His might that
His arrows may go swift and far. Let your bending
in the archer's hand be for gladness; For even as
He loves the arrow that flies, so He loves also the
bow that is stable." **By Khalil Gibran***

I trust that you have noticed the shift after reading
the above.

YOU ARE

enough

TO DO LIST & NOT TO DO LIST

TO DO LIST

PRIORITY	DUE DATE	WHAT	WHO	IN PROGRESS	DONE

TO DO LIST

PRIORITY	DUE DATE	WHAT	WHO	IN PROGRESS	DONE

THINGS TO DO TODAY

Date_________________________   **COMPLETED**

1) ____________________________________ ☐

2) ____________________________________ ☐

3) ____________________________________ ☐

4) ____________________________________ ☐

5) ____________________________________ ☐

6) ____________________________________ ☐

7) ____________________________________ ☐

8) ____________________________________ ☐

9) ____________________________________ ☐

10) ___________________________________ ☐

TO DO LIST

PRIORITY	DUE DATE	WHAT	WHO	IN PROGRESS	DONE

THINGS TO DO TODAY

Date_______________________ **COMPLETED**

1) _______________________________ ☐

2) _______________________________ ☐

3) _______________________________ ☐

4) _______________________________ ☐

5) _______________________________ ☐

6) _______________________________ ☐

7) _______________________________ ☐

8) _______________________________ ☐

9) _______________________________ ☐

10) ______________________________ ☐

TO DO LIST

PRIORITY	DUE DATE	WHAT	WHO	IN PROGRESS	DONE

THINGS TO DO TODAY

Date_________________________ **COMPLETED**

1) _________________________________ ☐

2) _________________________________ ☐

3) _________________________________ ☐

4) _________________________________ ☐

5) _________________________________ ☐

6) _________________________________ ☐

7) _________________________________ ☐

8) _________________________________ ☐

9) _________________________________ ☐

10) ________________________________ ☐

ABOUT THE AUTHORS

AS SEEN ON TV, RADIO & NEWSPAPERS

Tray-Sean Ben Salmi aka I'm That KID is not your average 14yr old. Tray-Sean Ben Salmi is a 14yr old Amazon No.1 Award Winning Author, Public Speaker Award Winning, Stock & Shares Trader, Property Investor, Presented award for TruLittle Heros Award 2018, Guest Speaker at The Best You Expo, Multi-award winning child advocate, Made For Mums Judge 2018, participated in campaigns for Sainsburys, Legoland, Warner Bros, Sony and Made For Mums to name a few, Child Genius 2017 1 of 20 smartest children in the UK, 1 of 34 boys invited to sit at the prestigious Eton College for Boys.

Official Judge for Made For Mums Toy Awards 2018 via Team Trouble, An award winning author of Kidz That Dream Big, Former Radio Show host, Regan Hillyer International Be Your Brand Fellow, Author of 10 Seconds To Child Genius, Winner of TruLittle Heros Award - Academic 2017, Public speaker, a business/personal developments mentor & coach and founder of I'm That KID Blueprint covers:

- I'm That KID - Bridging The Gap Between Fathers & Sons
- I'm That KID – Creating A Vision Board for My Future
- I'm That KID – Taking To The Stage
- I'm That KID - Inspiring My Community To Pay It Forward
- I'm That KID - There's A Book Inside ME
- I'm That KID - Families That Play Together, Stay Together
- I'm That KID - Empowering You To Step Into Your POWER
- I'm That KID - BEING The Change That I Desires To See In The World

And co-founder of 10 Seconds To Child Genius who is here to help child to plant the seed to create a brighter Future. Tray-Sean's signature program: I'M That KID Blueprint™

AS SEEN OF TV, RADIO & NEWSPAPERS

Lashai Ben Salmi aka DREAMPRENEUR is not your average 18yr old. She is a multi-award winning Youth Advocate, Presented award for TruLittle Heros Award 2018, Content Creator for The Korean Cultural Centre, Winner of TruLittle Heros Award - Entrepreneur 2017, Speaker at Virgin Money Lounge Historical Black History Month first ever event, Guest Speaker at The Beat You Expo, Guest Speaker at Mercedes Benz World 10th April 2018, High Profile Club, YouTuber with

25K plus subscribers and over 4M plus views (Korean Channel), An award winning author of Kidz That Dream Big, Andy Harrington ACE Coach, Former International Radio Show host, Winner of Regan Hillyer International Scholarship, a speaker, a business/personal developments mentor & coach, founder of Blossom Tree Photography & Videography produced content in association with Legoland Resort, Harry Potter, Little Mix and Disney Pixar, Sony, Warner Brothers & Universal etc, co-founder of A Precipice of A Dream and founder of Put The RED Card Up To bullying & My Journey - Giving Youth Several Reasons to Smile who is here to help children and youth to plant the seed for an abundance of unique opportunities via a variety of products and services to assist you to create a brighter future

Lashai has been mentored by some of the leading name within the personal development world Regan Hillyer, Andy Harrington, Cheryl Chapman, Harry Singha, Ralph Plumb, Sammy Blindell to name a few. Lashai has shared the stage with the likes of the late Dr. Miles Monrune, Dr. John Demartini, Andy Harrington, Robert G Allen and Ralph Plumb to name a few.

If you are looking for an inspiring, wise, talented, refreshing and powerful speaker then 18yr old Lashai Ben Salmi is guaranteed to make a big impact at your event. Lashai has been a part of the personal development world since the age of 11yrs. Lashai has a burning desire to transform lives with

her stage presence, knowledge and wisdom! Lashai's signature topics include: Congruency, Alignment, Self-Belief, YouTube, Social Media, Connection, Inspiration and Motivation.
Lashai's signature program: The Stepping Stone's Formula™
Book: Kidz That Dream Big: Dreams Do Come True
https://www.amazon.co.uk/dp/1912547066/ref=cm_sw_r_cp_api_mwbUAbS8BTQHE
Facebook page: Kidz That Dream Big:
https://www.facebook.com/Kidz-that-Dream-BIG-154694734627138/

BEN SALMI FAMILY MANTRA

BEN SALMI TEAMWORK MAKES THE DREAMWORK.
We believe that there is no such thing as failure only feedback.
We also believe that the journey of one thousand miles begins with a single step in the right direction

FAMILY ANTHEM

If you want to be somebody,
If you want to go somewhere,
You better wake up and PAY ATTENTION
I'm ready to be somebody,
I'm ready to go somewhere,
I'm ready to wake up and PAY ATTENTION!
The question is *ARE **YOU**?*

ABOUT OUR MENTOR DOUG PONSFORD

Doug Ponsford; has recently retired as the founder and managing Director of a successful IFA/Mortgage Broking Practice, which he setup back in the late 80's and is known as Henderson Ponsford & Co, employing a team of 6 Brokers and support staff.

It was in my teenage years when I discovered that I have an innate interest and a burning desire for knowledge in personal development. I knew then that I was to discover the secret behind our human potential.

Having firmly established himself and his company as a top player within the financial services arena, Doug turned his attention to purchasing property using creative financing methods which he had discovered whilst working as a specialist Mortgage Broker. This enabled Doug to Build a substantial property portfolio and setup Move on Now Ltd a company involved in buying, letting, trading and developing property for profit and has resulted in creating a well into six figure net passive income. Doug then set up and established a new company known as London Property University together with his business partner and for the past 4 years have dedicated his time to perfecting the cutting edge, niche strategy of Instalment Contracts, this has enabled Doug to massively grow his property business and substantially increase the number of properties that he now controls, whilst building a great team of fellow investors and partners. Having systemised the business with all legal documentation available at the press of a button, Doug's working partners, students and they are able to transact multiple sales and purchases with ease and in a timely fashion. Having studied most of the world leaders in Personal Development over the past 40 years, practiced their teachings and adopted the principles, his experience and coaching methods are unique, results driven and have a track record of achieving top class performance and high levels success. Doug is eager to share his knowledge and experience with those who are willing, show flair, and have the passion to succeed. Doug brings with him an excellent mix of in-depth knowledge and skills in the areas of property investing, personal development and business acumen. Utilising creative financing methods with a focus on instalment contracts, an easy to follow and apply personal development plan and award-winning business ethics. Doug looks forward to meeting and working with you and wishes you the greatest of joy and success in whatever you do.

Douglas Ponsford
Author, Investor, Public Speaker and Mentor

OUR JOURNEY

STEPPING
STONES
PUBLISHING
I
INFLUENCER
PUBLISHING
AWARD
winning
AUTHOR
YouTube

YOUNG CITIZEN
Nurturing the
special bond of
fathers and sons
Affordable Carpet

Star of the week

Tray-Sean Ben Salmi

Help

Salford

Tale of the boy, six, who ran
school short story contest

CLUBWEMBLEY.COM
CLUBWEMBLEY.COM
STAMFORD BRIDGE SW6
HOME OF
CHELSEA FC

Brother and sister inspiring young to follow their dreams
They pen book offering advice to budding entrepreneurs
Floyd & Son
DREAMING BIG TOGETHER
MAMAS
SECRET RECIPE™
How can you and your precious family learn how to
HAVE FUN, DREAM BIG & Make MONEY
doing what YOU LOVE?
SABRINA BEN SALMI
AND HER
FANTASTIC 5
MOTHER OF
THE YEAR
AWARD
WINNER
LASHAI AKA
TRAY-SEAN AKA
YASMINE AKA
PAOLO AKA
AMIRE AKA
AFFIRMATION
#1
"I AM
INTELLIGENT"
Amire Ben Salmi aka
Because I AM
Intelligent

V.I.P
V.I.P
V.I.P
V.I.P
V.I.
Global Authors' Award.
Think Global.
CHAMPION
2018
from Orkney to the Isl
of Wight. Talks, deba
Talk to us about
UK Parliament
Week 2017
UK
arliamentWeek
Engage. Explore. Empower.

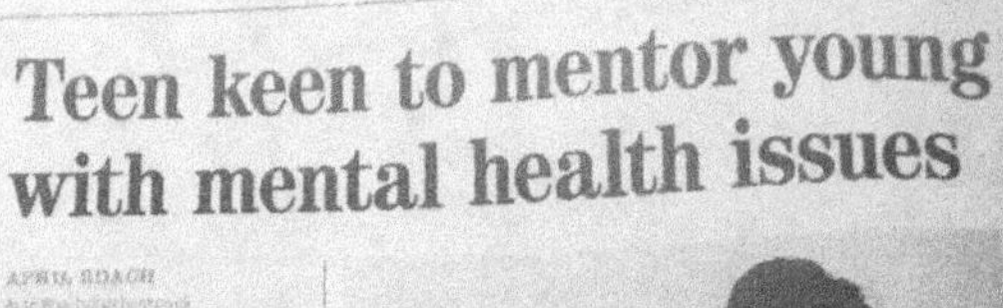

Teen keen to mentor young with mental health issues

An outspoken teenager from Romford is looking for two young people from the borough with mental health issues to take part in some mentoring sessions.

Lashai Ben Salmi, 17, from Barnstaple Road, has set up a competition for young people between the ages of 13 and 19, to send in their personal stories of why they could benefit from some mentoring.

The two winners will then have three one-to-one mentoring sessions with Lashai over three weeks.

Lashai told the Recorder: "I've seen an increase in mental health issues in young people, not just necessarily in this borough, but all over London.

"I work with a lot of young people who are under a lot of stress and are struggling with issues that may not be addressed by their school or at home, and I wanted to find ways to empower them.

"I would definitely say that extra pressures come from school. With the recent syllabus changes, more children are under a lot more pressure.

"Social media is another factor, as young people feel that there is a certain image they have to uphold."

Lashai has worked as a youth group leader and taken part in voluntary work with the National Citizen Service.

She has been inspired to work with young people after she suffered from bullying at a young age at school.

"This made me very passionate to help young people who might have gone through similar cases," she said.

Lashai added: "I've been involved in coaching young people before. So I wanted to raise awareness of what I do, but I also want to provide an opportunity to help two young people by mentoring them.

"In the mentoring sessions, I firstly try to understand the person and learn what's going on at home, at school and how any situations they may feel stuck in, can be changed. I try to find a compromise and provide them with stepping stones to get to where they desire to be."

To send in your stories for the competition, you can email Lashai at lashaibensalmi@ymail.com.

Lashai Ben Salmi is running a competition to find two young people from Romford to mentor.
Picture: KEN MEARS

YouTube Space
YouTubeSpaceLON
YouTube Space
YouTubeSpaceLON

YouTube Space
YouTubeSpaceLON
YouTube Space
YouTubeSpaceLON

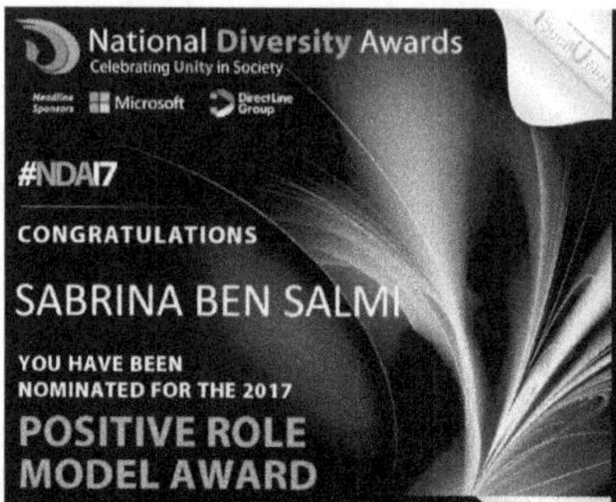
National Diversity Awards
Celebrating Unity in Society
Headline Sponsors
Microsoft
DirectLine Group
#NDA17
CONGRATULATIONS
SABRINA BEN SALMI
YOU HAVE BEEN
NOMINATED FOR THE 2017
POSITIVE ROLE
MODEL AWARD

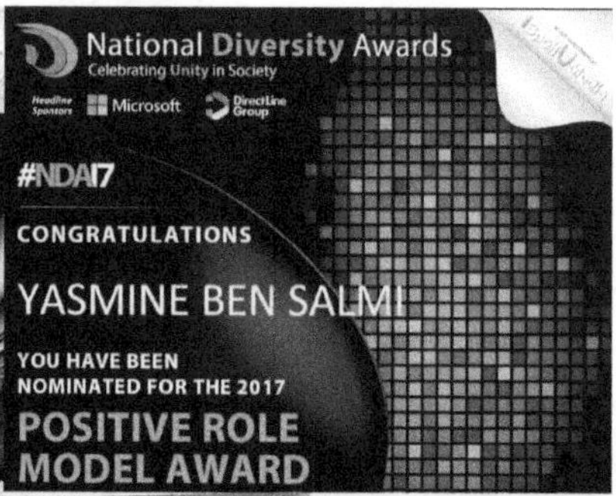
National Diversity Awards
Celebrating Unity in Society
Headline Sponsors
Microsoft
DirectLine Group
#NDA17
CONGRATULATIONS
YASMINE BEN SALMI
YOU HAVE BEEN
NOMINATED FOR THE 2017
POSITIVE ROLE
MODEL AWARD

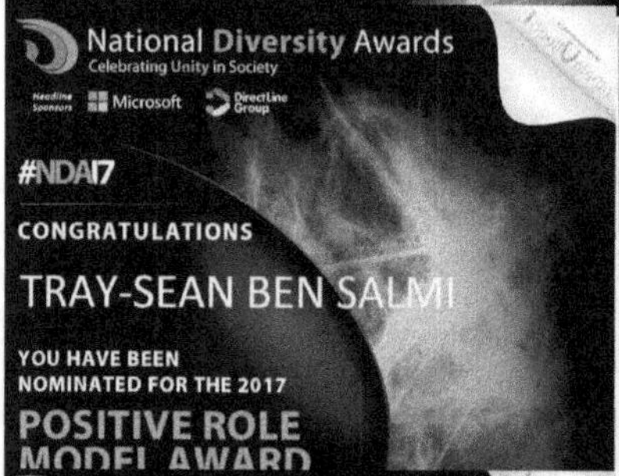
National Diversity Awards
Celebrating Unity in Society
Headline Sponsors
Microsoft
DirectLine Group
#NDA17
CONGRATULATIONS
TRAY-SEAN BEN SALMI
YOU HAVE BEEN
NOMINATED FOR THE 2017
POSITIVE ROLE

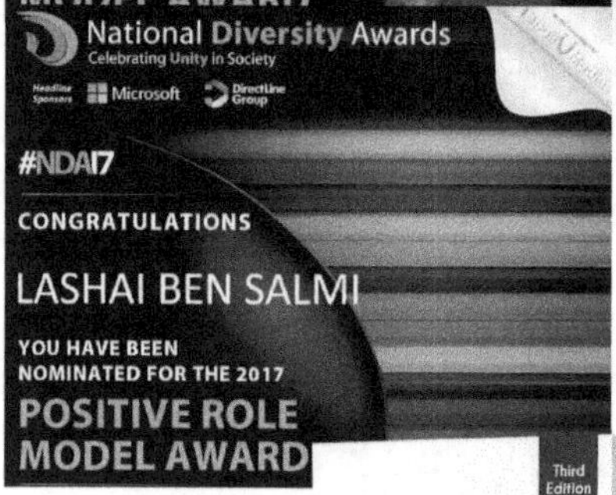
National Diversity Awards
Celebrating Unity in Society
Headline Sponsors
Microsoft
DirectLine Group
#NDA17
CONGRATULATIONS
LASHAI BEN SALMI
YOU HAVE BEEN
NOMINATED FOR THE 2017
POSITIVE ROLE
MODEL AWARD

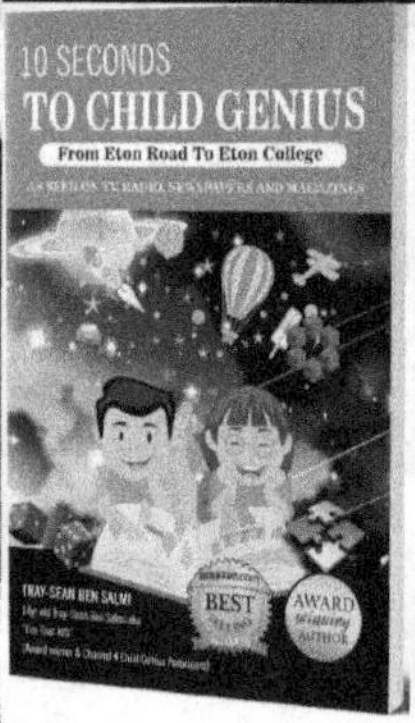
10 SECONDS
TO CHILD GENIUS
From Eton Road To Eton College
TRAY-SEAN BEN SALMI
BEST
AWARD

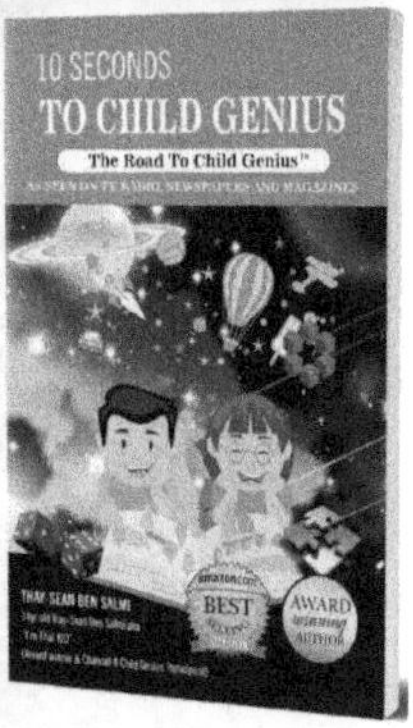
10 SECONDS
TO CHILD GENIUS
The Road To Child Genius™
BEST
AWARD

Third Edition
KIDZ THAT
DREAM
BIG
THE STEPPING STONES FORMULA™
LASHAI BEN SALMI
Foreword by ROBERT G ALLEN

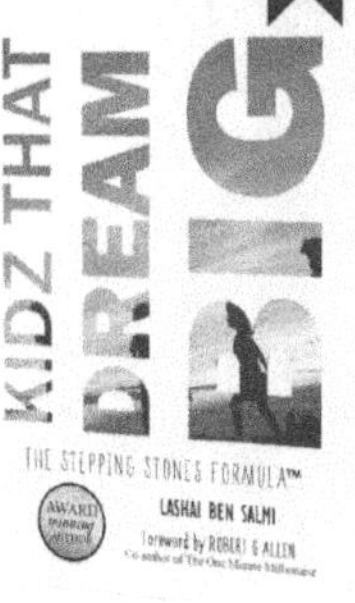

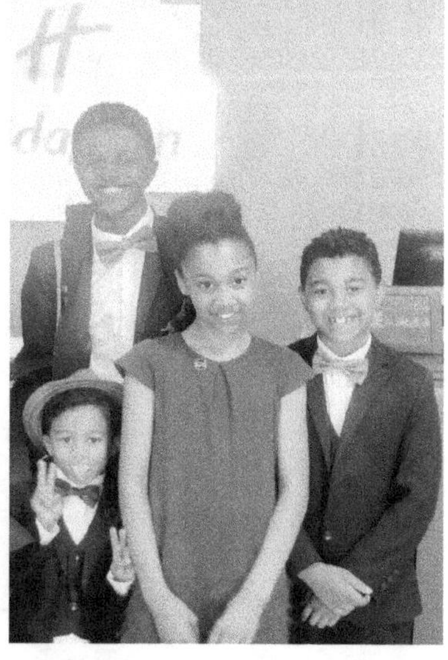

THE CHOICE IS YOURS
10 Key Principles
To Create A Happier Lifestyle
Yasmine Ben Salmi
sky
Ilford Recorder
BBC RADIO
THE BEST YOU
10 SECONDS TO CHILD GENIUS
BEST SELLING
AS SEEN ON TV, RADIO, NEWSPAPERS AND MAGAZINES
TRAY-SEAN BEN SALMI
13yr old Tray-Sean Ben Salmi aka "That KID"
(Award winner & Channel 4 Child Genius Participant)
PHILIP CHAN
& "10-Seconds Maths Expert"
Awards Winning Authors
METRO BANK
sky
Ilford Recorder
BBC RADIO
THE BIG ISSUE
UnLtd
THE BEST YOU

LONDON LIVE
Paolo Ben Salmi
ENTREPRENEUR
LONDON LIVE

10 SECONDS
TO CHILD GENIUS
From Eton Road To Eton College
AS SEEN ON TV, RADIO, NEWSPAPERS AND MAGAZINES
Second Edition
BEST SELLING AUTHOR
AWARD winning AUTHOR
TRAY-SEAN BEN SALMI
13yr old Tray-Sean Ben Salmi aka "I'm That KID"
(Award winner & Channel 4 Child Genius Participant)
&
PHILIP CHAN
"10-Seconds Maths Expert"
Awards Winning Authors
abc Forbes Entrepreneur CBS FOX NBC StarTribune The Boston Globe THE HUFFINGTON POST The Miami Herald
Tray-Sean Ben Salmi
Author, Speaker &
Coach
METRO SKY Recorder BBC RADIO THE BIG ISSUE UnLtd THE BEST YOU

SMYTH
LDN
Freelance Photographer
AS SEEN ON TV, RADIO, MAGAZINES & NEWSPAPERS ETC
AWARD winning AUTHOR
Third Edition
KIDZ THAT DREAM BIG
STEPPING STONES FORMULA™
LASHAI BEN SALMI & TRAY-SEAN BEN SALMI
Foreword by ROBERT G ALLEN
Co-author of The One Minute Millionaire
"I'M THAT KID"
MY JOURNEY
@lashaibensalmi & @traybensalmi
Kidz that dream big
Lashai Ben Salmi & Tray-Sean Ben Salmi

AS SEEN ON TV, MAGAZINES, RADIO & NEWSPAPERS

Inside this book the author will share woth you what he believes to be the difference when inspiring children and young people to strip into their power.

The author Tray-Sean Ben Salmi aka I'm That KID™ is not your average 14yr old. Tray-Sean Ben Salmi is a 14yr old Amazon No.1 Award Winning Author, Award Winning Public Speaker. Presented award for TruLittle Heros Award 2018, Multi-award winning child advocate, Memeber of Team Trouble (participated in campaigns for Sainsburys, Legoland, Warner Bros, Sony and Made For Mums to name a few) founded by Shadia Daho, Amazing Arabella & JD The Kid. Child Genius 2017 too smartest children in the UK. Official Judge for Made For Mums Toy Awards 2018 via Team Trouble. Tray-Sean is an award winning author of Kidz That Dream Big, Former Radio Show host. Regan Hillyer International Be Your Brand Fellow, Author of 10 Seconds To Child Genius, Winner of TruLittle Heros Award - Academic 2017, Public speaker, a business/personal developments mentor & coach and founder of I'm That KID covers: I'm That KID - Bridging The Gap Between Fathers & Sons™ (this was launched at Arsenal F.C), I'm That KID – Creating A Vision Board for My Future™, I'm That KID – Taking The Stage™, I'm That KID - Inspiring My Community To Pay It Forward™, I'm That KID - There's A Book Inside ME™, I'm That KID - Families That Play Together Stay Together™, I'm That KID - Empowering You To Step Into Your POWER™ and I'm That KID - BEING The Change That I Desires To See In The World™

I'm That KID™ is a book series. This book series aims to help children and young people to step into their power and holding going into life.

Always know that as long as you believe in yourself you can be, do and have whatever you desire.

I m That Kid
authortrayseanbensalmi
traybensalmi

Maxine's Shout

Inspirational message to kids

'Anything is possible' for proactive 10-year-old who designs own T-shirts

A 10-year old boy has designed his own range of T-shirts to publicise the importance of self-confidence in helping children reach their goals in life.

The message emblazoned on the back of the tops designed by Tray-Sean Ben Salmi reads: "I believe in myself and as long as I believe in myself I can do, be and have anything."

Tray-Sean was nominated for the Broxbourne Rotary Club Young Citizen Award last year with his sister Lashai for setting up an anti-bullying campaign after being victims at the hands of their peers in the school playground.

The cotton T-shirts, which cost £10 for boys and £8 for adults, are now available to the public.

Tray-Sean said: "I hope the message on my T-shirts will help children because when a child believes in himself anything is possible."

Tray-Sean's mother Sabrina, of Row Road, Hoard, said the family is pleased with the public response.

She said: "On Facebook and Twitter people have expressed how pleased they are with the positive tone of the T-shirts and there have been very supportive."

■ Follow @imthatkid2015 on Twitter; email imthatkidbytternasmie@gmail.com or call 07903 716123.

■ Mum Sabrina Ben Salmi with her children, from left, Lashai, 15, Paolo, six, Amire, two, Tray-Sean, 10 and Yasmine, seven.

CERTIFICATE OF
ACHIEVEMENT

This Certificate Is Awarded To

Tray-Sean Ben Salmi

For Dedication & Excellence
Child Genius Competition 2017

AWARDED BY

29th January 2017
DATE

LASHAI
BEN SALMI
15-16 FEBRUARY 2019
Olympia London
THE BEST YOU
expo
AMIRE
BEN SALMI
15-16 FEBRUARY 2019
Olympia London
THE BEST YOU
expo
YASMINE
BEN SALMI
15-16 FEBRUARY 2019
Olympia London
THE BEST YOU
expo
TRAY-SEAN
BEN SALMI
15-16 FEBRUARY 2019
Olympia London
THE BEST YOU
expo

CERTIFICATE
This Certificate Is Presented To
Paolo Ben Salmi
On Completion Of The March 2015
B.R.A.N.D. Kick Starter
www.brand-kickstarter.co.uk
#BrandKickStarter

CERTIFICATE
This Certificate Is Presented To
Yasmine Ben Salmi
On Completion Of The March 2015
B.R.A.N.D. Kick Starter
www.brand-kickstarter.co.uk
#BrandKickStarter

CERTIFICATE
This Certificate Is Presented To
Tray-Sèan Ben Salmi
On Completion Of The March 2015
B.R.A.N.D. Kick Starter
www.brand-kickstarter.co.uk
#BrandKickStarter

SURPRISE BONUS
WHICH AREAS OF YOUR LIFE NEEDS MORE

ATTENTION?

Are you **willing** to play full out? Yes or No?
Take a moment to honestly plot a dot to represent a

score from 0 - 10 on what is known as the 'Wheel

of Your Life'. 0 = totally unfulfilled and 10 = totally

fulfilled. I suggest that you make a copy of this

diagram, use a pencil or alternatively simply choose

three colours to perform one analysis at least every

three months, whatever suits you best. It is absolute

paramount that you allocate adequate time to reflect

upon each area of your life, to enable this process to

best serve you. Once you've a score for each area of

your life, simply join the dots (clockwise) to form a

full circle or whatever shape it forms. Remember

un-resourceful people do not exist, only un-

resourceful states and we both know that you are

the master of your mind... don't we? Yes or No?...

I want to remind **YOU**, that there is no such thing

as failure only feedback. However, it is your

responsibility to preserve the positive learnings for

yourself and for the future. This is an excellent

opportunity for you to pay close attention to the

areas needing to be improved - in order to restore

balance to your life. Fully consider what would

happen if you don't TAKE ALIGNED ACTION?

What did you learn from this process? What action

will you take today.

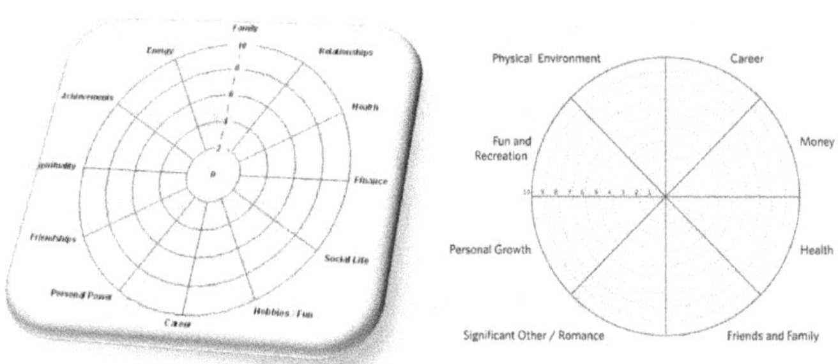

BONUS CHAPTER:
BE THE BEST YOU CAN BE

Convert your adversity into empowerment right here and right NOW. We believe that if you want to be the best you can be – it'll benefit you to create a pitch, build a network, convey gratitude, find a coach/mentor, build your profile, publish a book and create products/services. Allow us to explain in a little more detail:

- Pitch = know and communicate your message to your target audience with a burning desire.

- Network = in business it is not what you know or who you know that counts. What counts most is who knows you. Create and build good relationships with people who you like and trust, because this will enable you to gain exclusive JVs (joint ventures).

- Gratitude = always show gratitude for others, your health and opportunities. Respect will help you in your journey.

- Mentor/Coach = seek and you shall find... Get a coach, because a coach will expand your boundary conditions etc. Find someone who you would like to become or at least learn from.

- Profile = if you can't be found on the internet the chances are that people will not feel you are credible. What comes up when you type your name into any search engine? Create a trail leading to you and your mission.

- Publish = This change everything... when you become an author you gain credibility and visibility. The word author = authority *(SMILE)* writing a book is so much **FUN**

- Product = convert your knowledge, experience and skills into products for example: Books, Apps, Sweets, Cakes, DVDs, CDs, games etc

YouTube Space
YouTubeSpaceLON
PAOLO
BEN SALMI
15-18 FEBRUARY 2019
Olympia London
THE BEST YOU
expo

BENEFITS
OF EDUCATION
BENEFITS
OF EDUCATION

B.R.A.N.D.
KICK STARTER
CERTIFICATE
This Certificate Is Presented To
Lashai Ben Salmi
On Completion Of The March 2015
B.R.A.N.D. Kick Starter
www.brand-kickstarter.co.uk
#BrandKickStarter